oasis. definitely.

t i m   a b b o t

A Fireside Book
Published by Simon & Schuster

Fireside
Rockefeller Center
1230 Avenue of the Americas
New York, NY 10020

first published in great britain by
pavilion books limited

designed by josh eve and damian hale
project coordination by leesa daniels

typeset in helvetica 12pt
printed and bound in spain by bookprint

goodsexbaddrugsuglyrock'n'roll

*good*sexbaddrugsuglyrock'n'roll

fourwords

"your time has come"
noel gallagher, 1996

"who are the abbots?"
liam gallagher, 1996

Noel Gallagher (signature)

Liam Gallagher (signature)

"a book without pictures is a shit book"
liam gallagher, dublin 1996

to "our mams"

mum and dad,
liam, noel, bonehead,
guigs, and alan

and to the two chris's in my life
christine wanless and chris abbot

live forever

creation records was a ritualistic and strange, uncompromising culture. the ramshackle offices had withstood yet another ecstasy and jack daniels impromptu party. the company, which comprised various misfit geniuses, was well versed in abuse and the ceremony of smashing up the office at 5a.m., then re-opening at 10a.m. for business. this party had not been significant by normal standards, bar the words NORTHERN IGNORANCE, which had been scrawled in black marker pen across the reception's ceiling. the day after this extravaganza noel and liam gallagher came in and said that this label (particularly the ceiling) felt like home.

in 1993/94 the music of the world was the seattle/ generation x/grunge/wall of sound. the american influence in rock was domineering. britain could only answer back with the ineffectual mutterings of brett and his suedettes. it's easy to say you're the greatest rock 'n' roll band, however, one day you have to substantiate it.

the bunker was the ground-floor office that alan mcgee, dick green, and myself shared. we used to go though the overdrafts of alan's audio-visionary art statements. this entrepreneurial alliance never made hardcore money yet it was the last bastion of true independent music. music over money.

on the desk was the cassette box that stood out from the garbage bag of other hopefuls. on the box was a twisted spiral of the union jack with OASIS blocked out of the middle. liam commented, "yeah, man! this is the greatest flag in the world and it's just going down the toilet. we are going to be the biggest band in the world. we're british and it's just rock 'n' roll!" liam paced up and down the office like a caged leopard. noel ignored his brother's rants and got serious. he knew that creation was the right label, the right people, but it wasn't about money or the general music-business bullshit—it was about do you

BELIEVE?

soon to become ashen-faced youth and not so
youth—not a dry eye in the house. sign on the
dotted line
.... said a
corporate type.

good**sex**baddrugsuglyrock'n'roll

back from a vacation in portugal, in the comfort of his mom's back yard, the kid pulls the cover off a vintage '55 lambretta. bought a couple of years before for nothing, this is the kid's pride and joy and it means everything.

burnage, august '95

sticks and stoned could break your
bones but guigs will never
shake you

white here! white now!
cute, cheeky, chirpy, cockney
drummer chappy alan white gives
it large backstage at earls court.

earls court, november '95

after just completing the last of five tokyo dates, the band chill out and relax in the dressing room. oasismania had swept through japan and the fans' welcome had been outstanding.
taking it all in, the kid refreshes himself and takes control of the stereo. what did he play?
oasis.
who else?

liquid room, tokyo, september '9

happiness is a grape called gallagher

after all... you're

'5 PLUS

9   9A   10

longtime love is all you need.

bonehead and his longtime girlfriend kate.

good sex **bad** drugs ugly rock ' n ' roll

when you drink, swallow, and snort the music business, a quiet friday night indoors is a rarity. *definitely maybe* had beaten the much-touted, heavily marketed three tenors to the no. 1 album spot. it became the fastest-selling debut album ever. the week after its release the band jetted out to japan to the first signs of oasismania. from there they flew across the pacific to play seattle and san francisco. friday was the LA showcase gig at the whiskey a go-go.

mystery surrounds the methedrine mile that makes up sunset boulevard. from the chateau marmont (final home of john belushi's speedball) to the whiskey a go-go—infamous LA "rok" venue, home to primal scream's benefit night for the LA hell's angels earlier that year. across the road is the notorious viper rooms. in the middle of the meth mile is the mondrian hotel. the mondrian features in creation's rock 'n' roll history.

earlier that year—in February 1994—alan mcgee and myself had spent a night entertaining the LA indie clitterateri with our own style of bourbon 'n' bolivian room service. at 4:30a.m. LA was hit by its biggest earthquake since time began. not a recommended experience when on the tenth floor—out of it — watching the walls come tumbling down. there are better trips available.

seven months later another earthquake hit. this time it came in the shape of a phone call. in august 1994 noel called me at home in london; he was in LA. he said he'd had enough and had fired the band and could i call marcus (their manager) and arrange to have his guitars sent back to london? he said he'd be up for a night out when he got back from wherever he was going. at mid-day i boarded a flight to LA via denver. madder than *mission: impossible*. final destination unknown. for once the thought that noel wasn't invincible occured. why get this far so fast to fuck it off for one crap night?

entering room 411 in the mondrian i found the brain-fried remains of oasis. the scourge of methedrine mile had taken his toll. noel had had enough of the sloppy performance at the whiskey a go-go. the band were out of it. if the fans pay their money they get music, not twats who can't keep a tune. punches flew on and off stage. the chief, pissed off, left the gig and locked himself in his hotel room. the final straw came when a security guard used a pass key into his room. "are you noel gallagher?" asked the guard. maybe noel wasn't sure. time out.

sitting back in the room with the band it transpired that noel had quietly taken his passport, $1000, and a bag of pro-plus. for once even marcus, the steady controller, seemed miffed. how? why? where had noel gone? one scribbled phone number was the line, all there was to hang on to. the band didn't care about the band. even the kid was concerned about one thing only—noel. brothers are brothers. love is love.

the phone rang. it was a girl who might know where noel was. i told her if noel rang her, tell him to speak to us. by this time there was an FBI missing persons file open, airport checks. it was full on. the fugitive.

sweeter than any note ever played, came the guttural tones of noel on the line:
"what are you doing?"
"where are you?"
"i'm just having time in san francisco then getting back to london. the band's over."
"all right, i'll fly back with you."
"where are you?"
"i'm in LA you twat."
"ok. fly up to san francisco and then phone me and i'll give you the address. but don't tell anyone. i'm on my own."
flying halfway around the world without a destination is bizarre. not knowing what the state the person you're visiting is going to be in is even crazier.

the yellow cab pulled up in chinatown, san francisco. i was greeted by a beautiful oriental girl. she was later christened yo-yo gallagher, one of the unsung heroes of this mad week. in the main room of the apartment there was the chief. he had a ski sweater on in the middle of summer. the chief was in residence.

all british musicians i've worked with have a phobia about america. maybe this is part of the cultural divide. noel and i discussed this over the next few days. when you're sharing double rooms in america the tv defines the country's culture. flicking through the channels one morning we came across the ultimate talkshow competition—the pregnant beauty pageant. 11a.m., watching pregnant women in bikinis while having your cereal! c'mon, give the kids a break. noel looked at me, the brows said it all. this country's fucked. let's not let it fuck us some more. this was the turning point. when pregnant women in bikinis at breakfast dictate your state of mind, it's time to get out.
i suggested we just get out of san francisco. i've got plastic, we can go wherever we want. let's chill out. so we decided on some fear and loathing in las vegas. we were collected by cab from the coventry hotel where we'd been staying. the lunatic driver confirmed the US of A was the united states of aliens.

"going to the airport?" he asked.

"yeah," replied noel. "we're going to las vegas."

"nice. i've been there myself. gambling, shows, girls —a good time. excellent! the last time i went it was the annual alien observation society conference. of course, i've witnessed several UFOs—even a crash landing."

in the half-hour trip, the chief's brows dipped and danced through universal theories, philosophies, religious inca mysteries, psychic nonsense. this was the most overeducated taxi driver in the world. if he even was of this world. upon shaking hands with our alien leader, noel shot him down in one: "if you're that fucking clever, how come you're driving a cab? if you've got it, use it."

we arrived at las vegas early evening. noel's head was starting to take in this mad continent. it was a make-believe adult theme park. but everything that glitters is often hiding the mold. through several nights we battered through the grammage and litres like two men on a possible un-mission. time was irrelevant. light merged into darkness surrounded by twenty-four-hour day-glo heaven and hell. we talked about family, pets, shoes, bullshit and more bullshit, football, fighting, loving, bullshit and even more bullshit. all through this a game of telephone chess was going on as i informed marcus and friends that noel was fine, but didn't want to talk to anyone. at the same time the record companies with a stake were checking to see if their investment was secure. no, you twats, more like insecure.

the most annoying thing i ever heard from a record company was about somebody who had worked closely with kurt cobain: "i know he didn't like most of the promotion work we made him do. he felt compromised by the chinless, handshaking merry-go-round. but, wow, if we'd known he was going to do this to us, then maybe we wouldn't have worked him so hard." the public persona of all great stars is not their private disposition. they do not buy into compromise easily. noel is a perfectionist. focused and determined. another day, another dollar.

the time in las vegas was time to reflect on the madness of it all. the bigger you get, the bigger the thrill, the bigger the headache, the bigger the pill. i said to noel: "if john lennon left oasis he would have put out a farewell single, or at least finished the b-sides."

noel: "well, you might be right, but i can't face those fuckers."

me: "it's probably more the other way around. they know they've blown it. they just care about your head."

marcus rang—timing superb. the band had driven to austin, texas, on the off-chance that maybe the wanderer would return.

noel and i eventually decided to go to sleep for the first time that week. that afternoon we went for a walk. early evening we stuck into a jack daniels fest. opposite us was your traditional mid-american couple from missouri. the woman spoke up: "gee, can i just say to you guys, well i don't know how to say this but me and my husband, when we got married, we had a nuptial agreement that if ever i met george harrison, it would be all right if i slept with him. my husband wouldn't mind. well (looking the chief dead in the eye), can i just say i saw all the beatles' shows during the sixties and you're closest i'm ever gonna get to george."

several jack daniels later we staggered back to the hotel—alone! something had changed. noel said, "let's go to texas." as we walked through austin airport the unmistakable figure of producer owen morris bellowed out—"where the fuck have you been?"

we looked at each other—

BELIEVE.

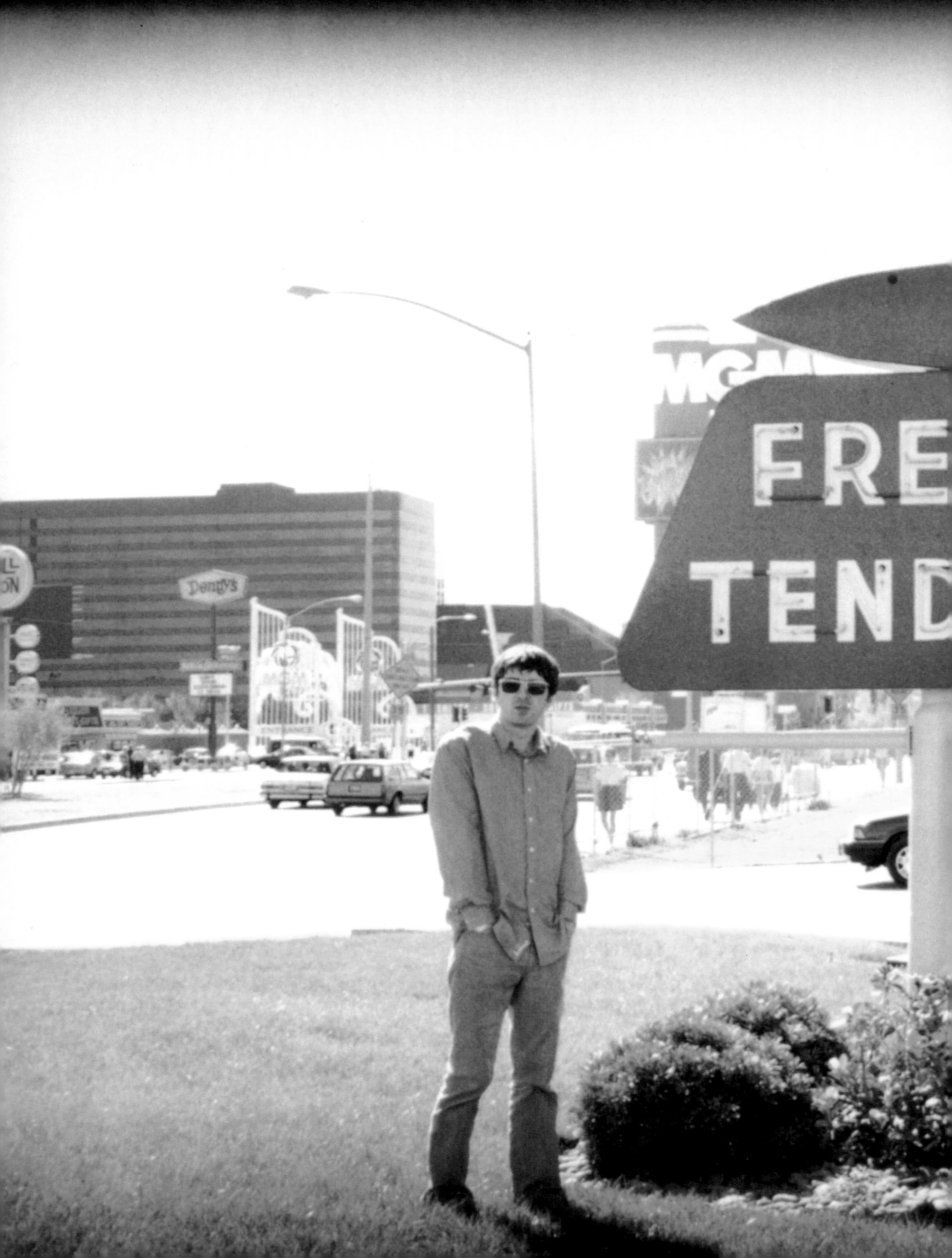
MGM
Denny's
FRE
TEND

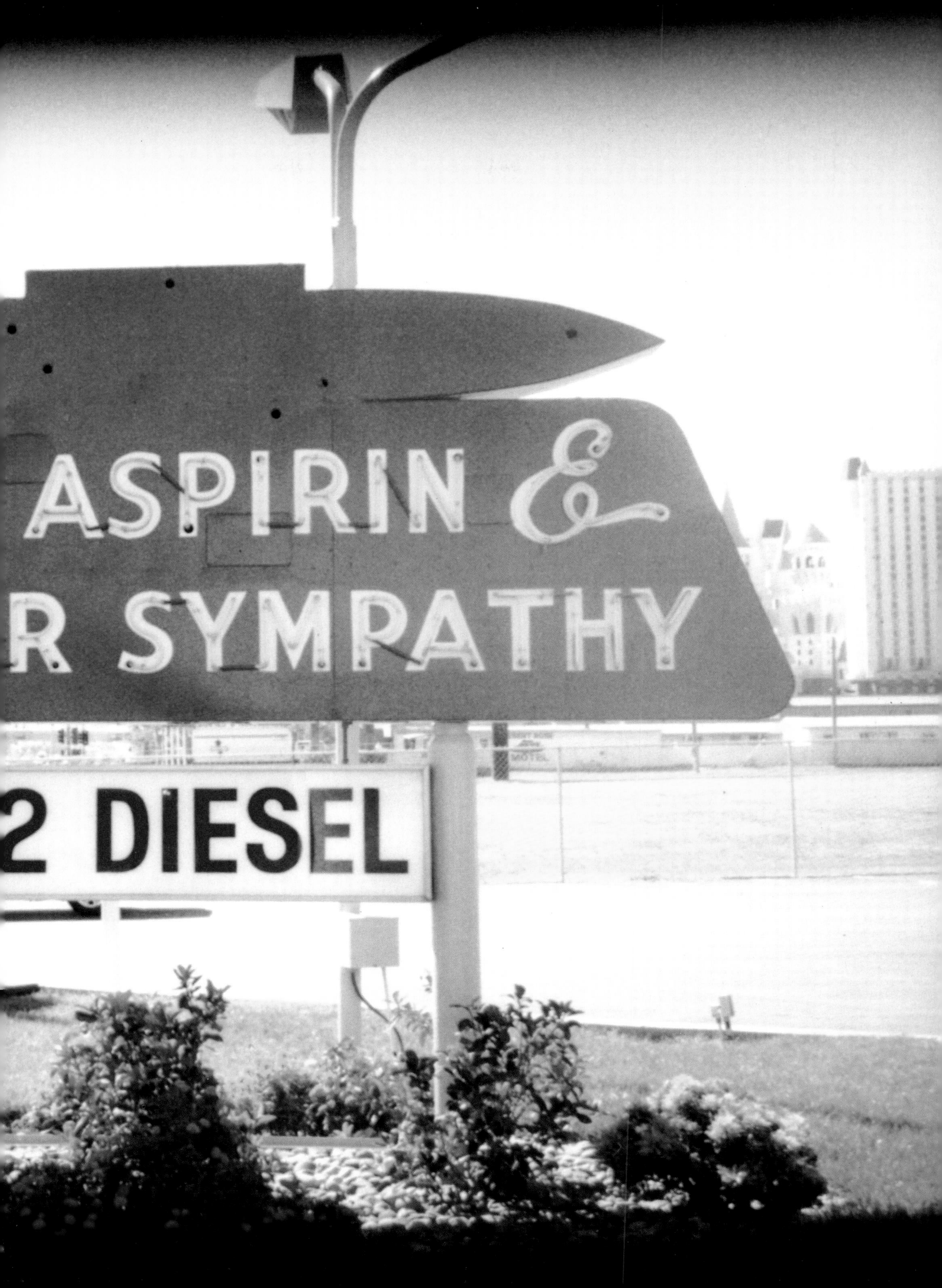
ASPIRIN &
R SYMPATHY
2 DIESEL

scott mcleod will probably be remembered as the pete best of oasis. with guigsy recuperating from exhaustion at a time when not only an english and european tour loomed, it was imperative to find a replacement. scott was an old acquaintance of the band. he was already playing in a manchester group called the ya ya's, and after a quick start into the live dates, things seemed to be running smoothly. the promise of girls, drink, travel, and the jet-set lifestyle did not appeal to young scott. he couldn't settle and felt the pressure was too much. in america, with dates to complete, scott approached margaret, the band's tour manager, and told her he was leaving. he refused to get on the tour bus and couldn't be coaxed into changing his mind. scott caught the plane home, without saying goodbye. when told the news that scott had left, oasis responded the only way they could—they laughed.

tony mccarrol's departure from the band came, inevitably, after a fracas with liam in paris in april '95. the writing had been on the wall for some time. tony had been a member of liam's original band, rain, where he played competently for that level. with noel's arrival in oasis and his demand that everyone give 100 percent all the time and have a total dedication to the band, tony began to feel the pressure. while everyone else accepted the new discipline and commitment, tony seemed to struggle. everybody's musicianship improved, but a divide was growing between tony and the other members. with the success of the first singles, a growing reputation as a dynamite live act, the impact of *definitely maybe*, and a growing fan-base in europe, japan and the united states, it was becoming clear that oasis were going supersonic. during this time it was stressed to tony that his drumming needed to improve. guigs and bonehead were developing their own styles, the kid's vocals were getting more defined, and noel was on his way to becoming one of the most influential songwriters of his generation. it was felt that tony hadn't progressed with them. internal strains were starting to show, both personally and musically. it all came to a head after a night in paris. an argument between liam and tony escalated into a punch-up and it was now clear that the situation could no longer continue. noel gave the nod and tony was told he had to go—which he did with no fuss or fanfare.

out   of   the   b a d   c o m e s   g o o d

a new era beckoned: oasis with alan white. alan white brought a whole new dimension to the dynamic of oasis. he was eager to learn and improve his own talents and, more than anything, wanted to be in oasis. alan had already auditioned for another band on creation, and alan mcgee was impressed enough to tell noel about him. noel called alan and asked him to audition. he was the only person noel asked to play. the job was his. alan fitted into the band immediately. his first job, three days after he joined, was playing on *top of the pops* to "some might say." his first big gig was playing in front of ninety thousand people at glastonbury. nice work if you can get it!

paul "guigs" mcguigan is probably the quietest and most elusive member of oasi self-taught bass player, guigs was an origi member of rain and an old friend of bonehead.

maybe it's shyness but guigs's introvert exterior hides a man who applies himself anything and makes sure he excels at everything.

as a boy, guigs was a greater manchester junior boxing champion. he's an excellent footballer with a knowledge about the gam that's second to none. he's also a formidal cricketer. guigs makes sure that anything does, he does his best.

in a way he is removed from the other members of the band. although always "m for it" he will be the one reading a book or sugar ray robinson as well as a novel abo the moss side massive.

if it's the little things that make you so hap then guigs is the perfect example. unfazed the glitterati, he will give you an evening o in-depth analysis on the history of manche city, recall the events of a tyson fight, talk about the preparation of a japanese sushi dish, and then teach you how to play your favorite song on acoustic guitar.

it's this quiet, sensitive personality that too battering when the oasis rollercoaster ride started. the whole band felt the pressure o being involved with becoming one of the world's biggest bands. constant touring around the world, recording, relentless pre obligations, not being able to see your friends or family—there is only so much yo can take.

one day, in august 1995, after recording *(what's the story) morning glory?*, headlinii glastonbury, returning from a successful to in japan, guigs decided that he couldn't do any more. something had snapped and he never wanted to pick up his guitar again. h told the band he wanted to leave, and they were stunned. it was this news that stoppe the madness that had been happening wit the band. everyone came to their senses a remembered the reason why they had got together in the first place—to make music, have a laugh, and share the good times w each other. they realized that much of this had been lost and they had begun to drift apart. it was guigs's announcement that bought oasis back to what they had been the very start—a family; an untouchable u whose members look after one another.

guigs was told to go and rest and when he was ready to return he could. so guigs spe the next two months sleeping, going fishin with his friend jeff, and spending time with girlfriend ruth. it was exactly what he need while the rest of the band went touring in t united states, guigs got his head together. triumphant return came at the massive ea court gigs in november 1995. not only did band look complete once again, but the reception guigs got from the fans was immense and highly emotional. he was ba

liam has just finished recording "champagne supernova" and he wants to go out and celebrate today's result (blackburn beat manchester united). their producer, owen morris, and noel are telling him he has to stay in ...

owen: "i think that vocal was good but i think we could do better."
liam: "well, let's leave it then."
owen: "you need to rest your voice and stuff because you *can* sing better."
liam: "we can leave it for another time."
owen: "oh yeah, i don't think we should do it tonight because you'll sound exactly the same. so lay off the cigs and booze for a bit."
liam: "leave it out, man."
owen: "lay off all the things you enjoy, liam."
liam: "oh come on, blackburn won. i've got to go out and have a laugh."
owen: "you don't even support blackburn!"
liam: "but i hate fuckin' man u big time."
noel: "we've got an album to do here. there's more important things to do."
liam: "oh, i'll be chilled tonight."
noel: "no you won't. you'll come back at six o'clock in the morning and you won't be able to sing it and i'll get *really* pissed off."
liam: "so what have i got to do? stay in tonight?"
noel: "if you stay in, i'll stay in."
owen: "i'll stay in."
noel: "i'll stay in and work. i'm not having a day off."
liam: "that's what i mean, you're gettin' your kicks out of work and i'll be sat here."
noel: "the point is you should be gettin' your kicks out of fuckin' gettin' your voice together."
liam: "i can do that. i'll be able to fuckin' do that, man. i've got to go out for a couple of drinks. i won't smoke ..."

owen: "listen, right."
liam: "no, you listen to me, i won't be smokin'."
owen: "no, for the end of the first week of the session your voice is in bad nick, right. so you need to chill a bit and get your voice back."
liam: "it's always fucked."
owen: "it's not that fucked. it sounds like you've been singing for four weeks."
liam: "it's because i was out last night."
owen: "exactly!"
liam: "i'll just go out for a couple of jars and i'll be in at twelve. honest to god!"
owen: "but when you go out you gabber."
liam: "i won't gabber tonight."
noel: "pick a number, with as many notes at the end as you want."
liam: "what?"
noel: "if you go out tonight, you won't shut up talkin' because that's what you do best."
liam: "i'll go for two and then i'll be back here."
owen: "it is pretty serious though. you've got to calm down with your voice. you've spent half of today shoutin'."
liam: "because of the football."
owen: "but it is kinda everyday, though. you obviously know it's your responsibility, your voice."
liam: "so what are you saying?"
noel: "so what you're saying is, fuck it!"
(liam starts playing the guitar. noel and owen ignore him and get back to work.)

within a minute liam puts the guitar down and saunters off to one of monmouth's drinking establishments … not giving a damn!

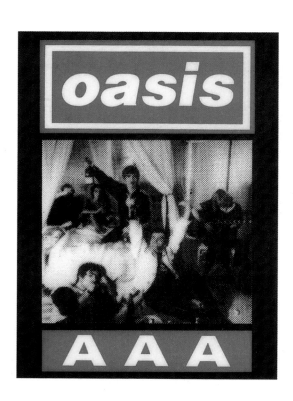

good sex bad **drugs** ugly rock 'n' roll

"cigarettes and

15   ▷ 15A   16   ▷ 16A   17   ▷ 17A
20   KODAK 5054 TMZ   21   KODAK 5054 TMZ   22   KODAK 5054 TMZ

20   ▷ 20A   21   ▷ 21A   22   ▷ 22A
Z   25   KODAK 5054 TMZ   26   KODAK 5054 TMZ   27   KODAK 5054 TMZ

25   ▷ 25A   26   ▷ 26A   27   ▷ 27A
Z   30   KODAK 5054 TMZ   31   KODAK 5054 TMZ   32   KODAK 5054 TMZ

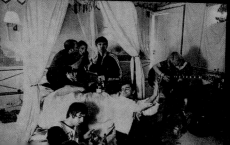

alcohol'

▷ 18A   **19**   ▷ 19A
KODAK 5054 TMZ   24   KODAK 5054 TM

halcyon hotel, london, august '94

it became evident that the only way to portray "cigarettes and alcohol" was to epitomize what life was becoming. let's get the best hotel in london, the best room in the hotel, the best wine and spirits from the bar, the best women, the better people, the better class "a"s and get cabin fever. michael spencer jones directed by brian cannon shot the rolls in the 72nd hour. the bar bill and damage deposit up for negotiation - a hasty exit was made in the 73rd ...

▷ 23A   **24**   ▷ 24A
KODAK 5054 TMZ   29   KODAK 5054 TI

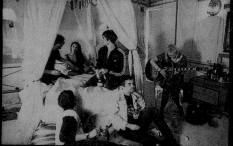

▷ 28A   **29**   ▷ 29A
KODAK 5054 TMZ   34   KODAK 5054 TM

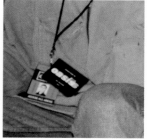

tokyo, late september, and the heat
and humidity of the city are
oppressive. the heat on stage is
overwhelming. every show has been
riotously received by the normally
sedate japanese audiences, but now,
after the show, is the time to chill out.
jason rhodes, noel's guitar roadie,
mans the megaphone, a toy he has
played with all week. bonehead,
guigs, and alan unwind, recounting
anecdotes from the night's show.
noel shares jokes and stories with
celebrated manchester dj/producer
justin robertson, who just so happens
to be in japan as well. liam and noel
used to visit justin's club, most
excellent, in manchester. now they
share time in oasis's dressing room
in japan. funny old world.

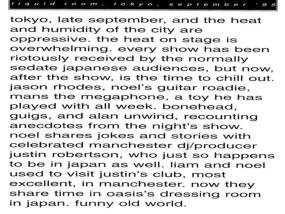

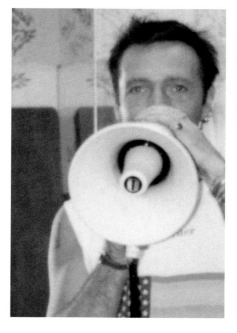

liquid room, tokyo, september '95

although renowned around
the world for making excellent
electronic goods and fine
automobiles, the japanese
have never been among the
most gifted dancers. this
mysterious fellow appeared in
the dressing room and began
to throw down some moves,
but that old smoothie, noel,
takes to the floor and
obliterates all competition.
nice little mover.

C'MON THE BURN
manchester united set their sights
on the double double.

THE MAINE GAME
down tools on recording "morning
glory." 3p.m. kick off to decide the
fate of the red foe. bonehead the
well-cut man united supporter
finally gives in to taunting from his
blue-loving colleagues. c'mon the
burn, c'mon the hammers. the
news from upton park is definitely
not good for bonehead. the blue-
nose celebrations start as the final
countdown begins, then guigsy
interrupts, it's gonna be all over.
redknapp fires the spark and
boots one into the back of the net
and bang goes man united's
dream. back at rockfield fire
extinguishers go off. tables turn.
"c'mon, you bald fucker," they cry.
penny and owen morris drink all
the way through it. have joy and
we have rockfield on the run.
soccer glorious soccer.

the men responsible for the doubleworthy *help*—bosnia—record recruit the brothers grin—andy and tony, we salute you

lend's a quid—your checks are in the mail—mcgee/burger with major asset

"have you heard, it's in the stars. next july we collide with mars. well, did you ever! what a swell party this is!"

the mercury music awards was yet another burning night out. with everyone suited and booted, the whole gang was ready to roll. it was the most raucous table in the room, no. 1, no less. oasis were up for best album of the year with *(what's the story) morning glory?*. yet, when portishead won it for *dummy*, table no. 1 gave them a standing ovation. everyone was having such a good time that at one point, when oasis were asked to come onto the stage, they were too busy chattering to realize. when they did eventually make it up there, their speech was a rendition of the evening's menu. it didn't matter who had won, everyone just relaxed and partied, happy to see other people happy. so much so that liam was one of the last people to leave the post-awards party, serenading anyone he could on a white grand piano.

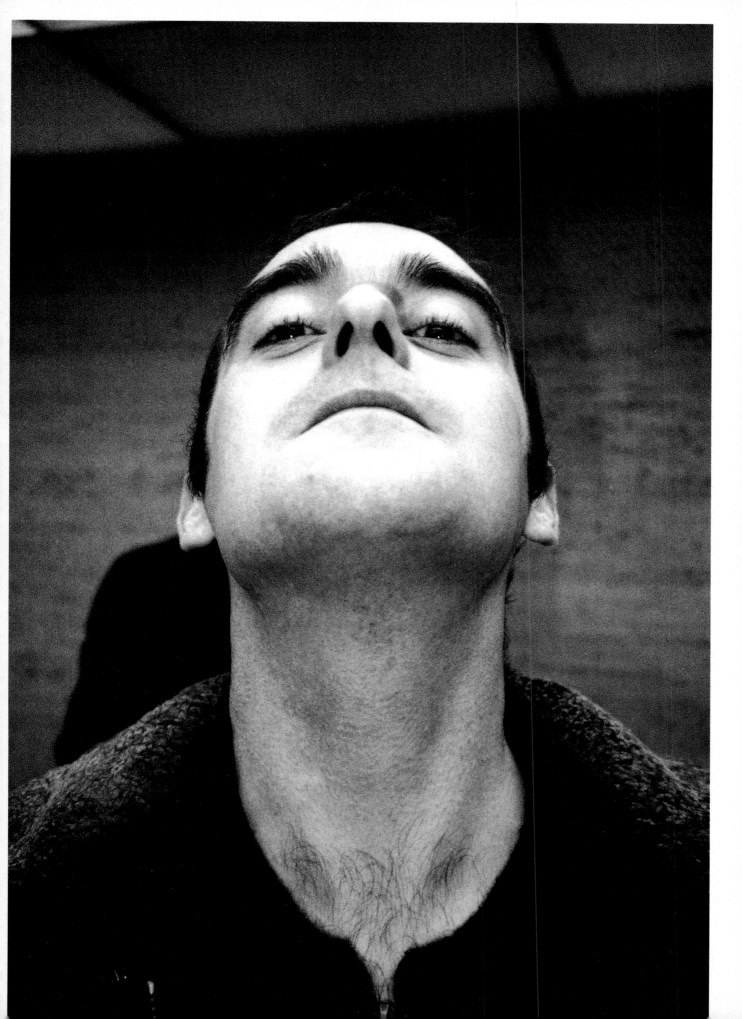

(bono and peggy gallagher have a
heart to heart)
this was the weekend in dublin i
would never swap for the world; with
family and friends gathered to
celebrate oasis. the atmosphere that
had captured dublin was incredible!
out front and backstage it was
electric. when noel began
wonderwall, he strummed the first
chords and the whole place sang
with him, bringing a tear to his eye.
the warmth and good feeling of that
weekend was truly memorable.
outside, for £1, you could purchase
stick-on gallagher "monobrows."
backstage, steve collins, bono, the
edge, family and friends all
mingled together. total blarney.

"i'll tell you about the bible —there's no pictures in it. how can you buzz off a book, right, without no pictures in it? you've got to have one picture floating about. if there ain't no pictures in a book, you can fuck right off!
i want to see jesus getting off his tits and smashing the stalls up. i want to see jesus walking on wine ... or whatever, walking across water going, 'waaahhyy, i'm a geezer.' but there's no pictures to prove it. so fuck right off. there's no pictures to prove that jesus turned water into wine, i know he did and i know he's a geezer, but a book without pictures is a shit book."

(pulls out chain with crucifix attached)
"this symbolizes that there is four ways to life. there's upstairs, downstairs, the man who lives to the left, and the man who lives to the right. and that's what it's all about. because if people believed in one fucking thing, we'd all wear circles. there's four ways to each fucking ... hedgehog! so it's like upstairs, downstairs, left, right, and who's in the middle? the kid! so put that in your fucking pipe and fuck right off! it don't mean nothing but it means something."

the weekend when you really could say to your best mate, "got a boss photo of your missus the other night." family shenanigans, and mamas and papas sent to bed early—not everybody made it to mass that morning, but as every good altar boy knows, the best service is in the evening. and even the bosnian foreign minister showed up!

eyebrows down. outside the point, entrepreneurial
punters start a line in stick-on monobrows, pund a
piece. where gallagher meets groucho, it all goes
pear-shaped.

a real st. patrick's celebration with mints all round

as fields go, the fields belonging
to michael eavis are top fucking
fields. this weekend was very
important in many ways. it brought
together a lot of people who became
firm friends. it was oasis's biggest
gig to date and it confirmed their
position as one of britain's biggest
bands. glastonbury celebrated the
rise of pulp and marked the
unfortunate decline of the stone
roses, who were scheduled to play
but pulled out. it was an out and out
party, a nerve-tingling rollercoaster.
starting with trepidation, leading to
degradation, and ending with
levitation. well, it wouldn't be
glastonbury without a bit of that, man.

during the glastonbury weekend, bonehead celebrated his thirtieth birthday. the band's caterers baked him a birthday cake and presented it to him. pictured here are mouse, the caterer, kate — bonehead's girlfriend — and the man himself.

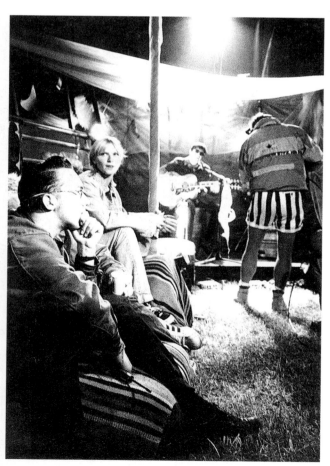

"hi, it's saturday night, live from glastonbury.
i'm mark lamarr and she's jo whiley. we're
all buzzing and i have robbie williams from
take that here, and noel gallagher over
there."

"so, robbie what the hell are you doing here?"

noel: "right, seeing as though no one cares about what i'm doing, i'm off."

noel: "oh, hold on a minute, i'll say something if they like it or not. 'hello mam!'"

liam likes a sleep

"coz people believe they're gonna get away for the summer. why, why, why, why?"

earls court . london . nov '95

earls court warm-up
sees wig-hat farrago. a
melon-twisting outfit.
suits you, sir.
splendid, said the crowd

funky moped

earls court , london , november '95

RALLY BACK
no turbans for these young scooter enthusiasts. brand new — italy's finest shopping transport ferries
guigs fresh from a spot of fishing to earl supernova's earthquake. a mohican for guigs and a mower
for bonehead.

the bootleg lennon-lookalike
winners

earls court , london , nov

if ever there were pictures tha
dismissed all those ludicrous
tales about the band's nasal
abuse, here they are (right).
treats his hooter with all the
care and attention you would
puppy. bless.

good sex bad drugs *ugly* rock'n'roll

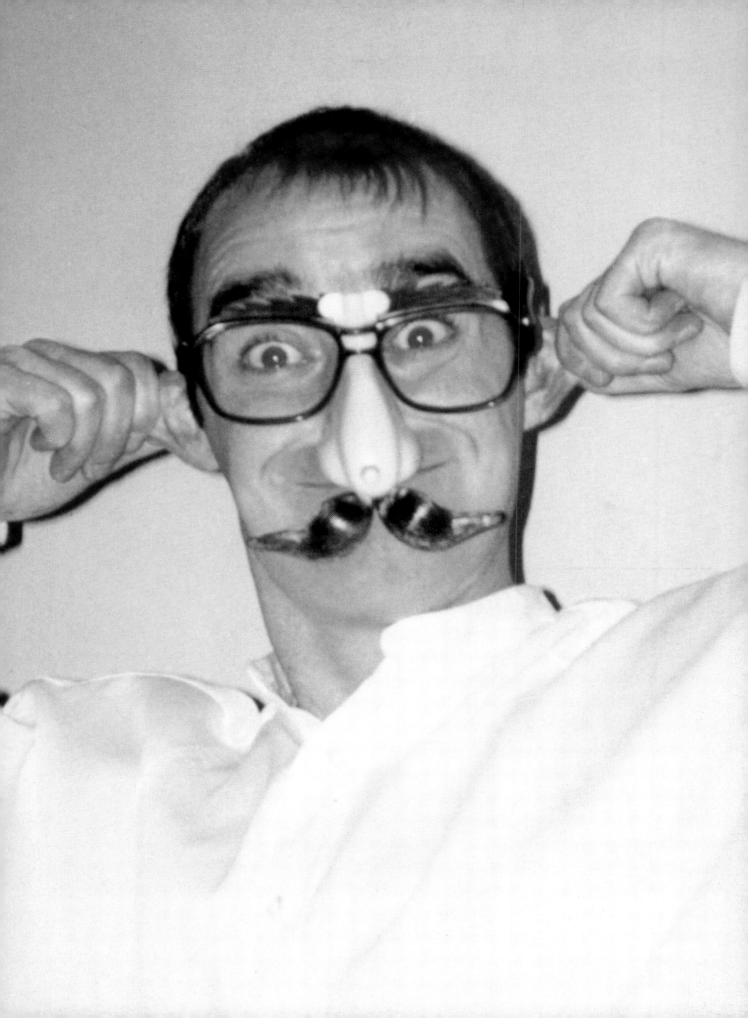

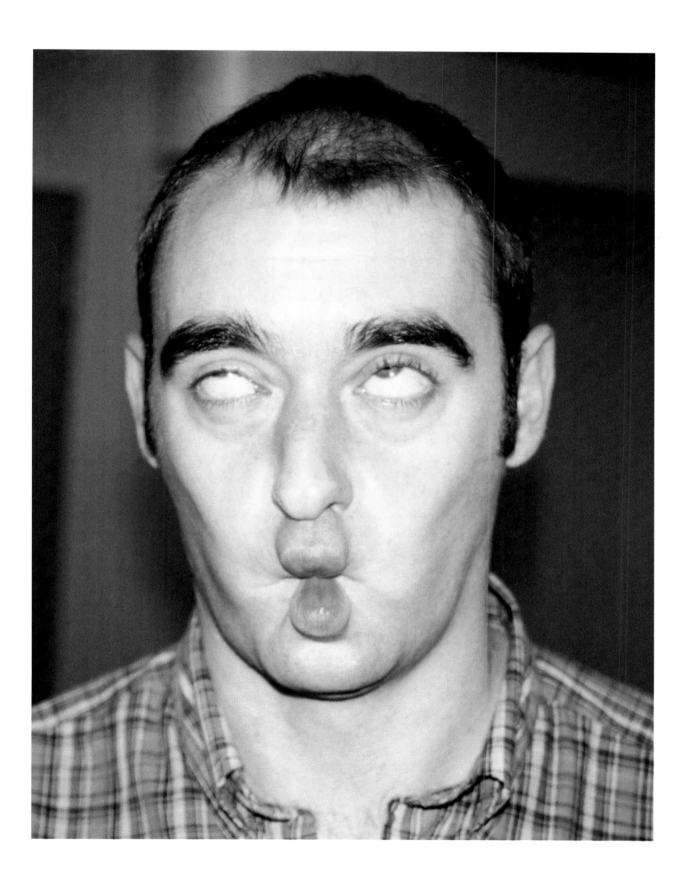

"you can pick your manager and you can pick your nose, but you can't pick your manager's nos

answers on a postcard.

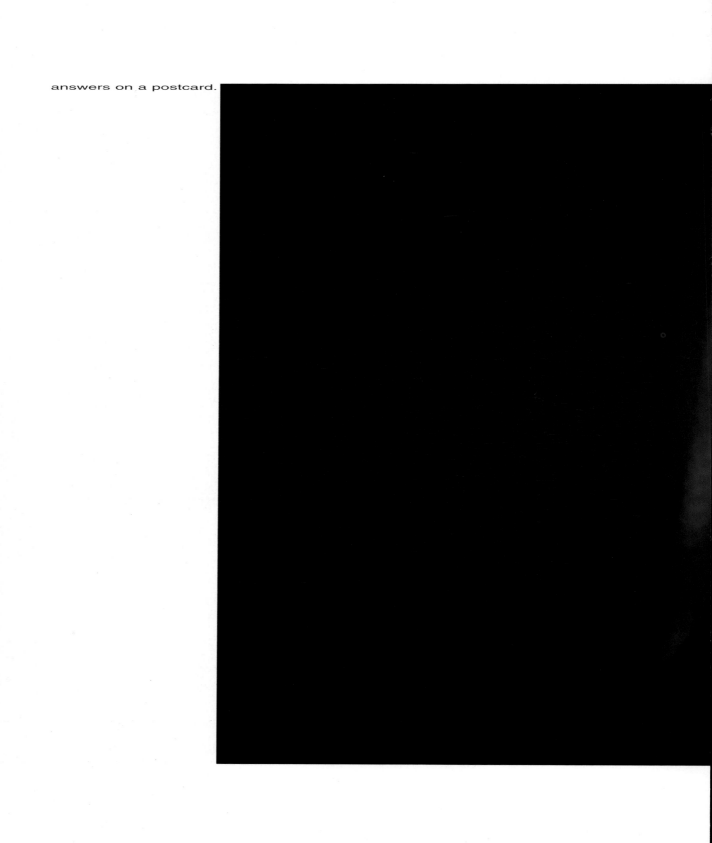

melissa
queen of indie merchandizing. snowboarding,
bong-head american, folded more fivers and
t-shirts than marks & spencers. musical tastes:
absurd swampabilly.

jason
just because you're a character doesn't necessarily
mean you have character—solid gold. noel's guitar
man, last to bed, first up, this man is a chemical
impossibility.

phil
wore his sky-blue top from day one. early hero of
world tours, slipped off for the "second coming".
one part of hinge and brackett alongside that
other original—"the world is yours" mark coyle.

roger
the other half of the keighley cougars.
known to few as the mod hod.

margaret
tour manager—great job. amazing balls for a
woman, total worker, never known to lose it and
was once spotted sharing a joke after hours.

sid
sid, daryl, coates, martin. a cast of
thousands, the red oasis in a sea of
blue. champagne lifestyle, lemonade
income. when sid says he'll be there,
he was there!

alan—the president
in the words of vivian stanshall "a right hooly ginger geezer." he came, he saw, he signed, he conquered. the definitive indie entrepreneur, from british rail clerk to multi millionaire, scottish as bannockburn, still does the lottery and he'll probably win again. his dad, john, is crazy, sixty going on sixteen—the oldest member of creation, forever a jake, never a flake. respect.

tricky dicky
ung hero of creation, known to go a bit
ly on his third case of pils, best time to
im to sign a check. always there from
sands of time. once spotted on top of
pops with the jesus and mary chain,
now a happy rural family man.

j.p. and stu
men in suits often seen to
loosen their ties. occasionally.
responsible for sowing
creation's success in a
corporate style. actually like
music.

johnny
earliest supporter. the terror of
many a journalist. his press
masterplan was second to none.
even saw off the three tenors.

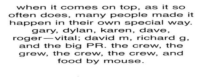

when it comes on top, as it so
often does, many people made it
happen in their own special way.
gary, dylan, karen, dave,
roger—vital; david m, richard g,
and the big PR. the crew, the
grew, the crew, the crew, and
food by mouse.

marcus
the daffy taffy. a true music-business
entleman, mr. marcus russell, leader of the
gang—ignition, cool, calm, and collected.
favorite saying—arsed!

brian
C'MON the cannon. be trusted!

BONEHeaD

cable tv show , canada , '95

after a busy schedule of interviews, meet-and-greets, and formal conferences,

noel and bonehead take to the streets of tor

NOEL

ed with their guitars and a television camera crew they give an
impromptu rendition of *live forever* to a more than receptive crowd.

14 3 1995

traveling to amsterdam for the
weekend. the away firm is topped up
as ever by crazy brits and inter-rail
mcdonald's thieves. top girl supplied in
the shape of a young girl named meg
matthews, and seventy-two hours of
soccer boots and away strips courtesy
of kadamba—god damn her!

'Calling out around the...

... world, are you ready...

...for a brand new beat.'

the paramount picture session rounded off the east coast promotions and
decided how the west would be won.

it's a great life on the buses! the tourbus becomes house and home for its fifteen occupants on the road for as long as six weeks. these beautiful carriages have twelve bunks with hot/cold air-conditioning —one minute you're freezing, the next you're roasting. the tourbus also has a living room complete with tv, video, stereo, and nintendo. the eating area is at the front of the bus. it has a special refrigerator packed with beer. the man with dark glasses on is producer mark coyle: he's great first thing in the morning.

the musical mystery tour starts off as fun but after about three weeks tempers can get frayed. a "crispy" (tantrum) is allowed from time to time, but one rule that must be observed all the time is—"no logs in the lav!"

after each stop in a new city the band's living room would fill up with yet more swag and memorabilia: hard-to-find records, obscure john lennon interviews, badges, bags, and boxes. by the time you leave the bus your bunk is that crammed with so much shit that you sleep in a cramped corner. not that that matters; after each gig everyone gets stupidly drunk and stoned before retiring to their respective berths.

truckstops and fast food become the norm.
after rehydrating first thing in the morning,
the belly rumbles. a big mac, large fries,
and twenty chicken mcnuggets are
promptly ordered. have a nice day. bonjour.

nellee hooper, the producer,
super-duper ligging smoocher. the
kid wrestles with the two loves of
his life—guitars and patsy.

bow . london . '95

morning glory video shoot way out in bow, east london. it saw the american release not as early out of the traps as first predicted. a film, no less.

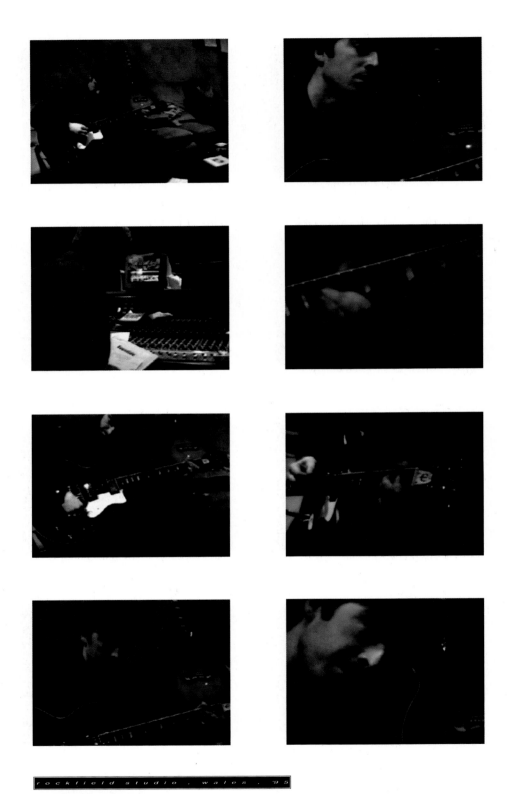

rockfield studio . wales . '95

noel puts down
"champagne supernova"
krug style for the first time
ever as the kid's premix
vocal was clearly different
from anything he'd done
before. if he screamed his
way through "definitely
maybe" then the kid
definitely sang "morning
glory."

chris abbot and noel spend a night reminiscing about noddy holder and slade—a b-side develops in twenty-four hours. anyone still standing is drafted in for backing vocals—put your boots on, skinhead.

"the one thing oasis and blur have got in common is that we're both not doing very well in america." damon albarn of blah! richard griffiths and david massey, the anglophile heads of epic records, rewards to the conquerors with "their not very well done" two million platinum disks backstage at a sell-out madison square gardens. as ever the kid is out buying old school running shoes, having shaken one hand too many for the day.

"no one's my fuckin' competition, and it's the truth. call me this, call me that, i don't give a fuck. i know for a fact we are the fuckin' real deal. they ain't seen the likes of it ever. not twenty years, thirty years, forty years. i'm on about ever."

elvis? fuck 'im!"

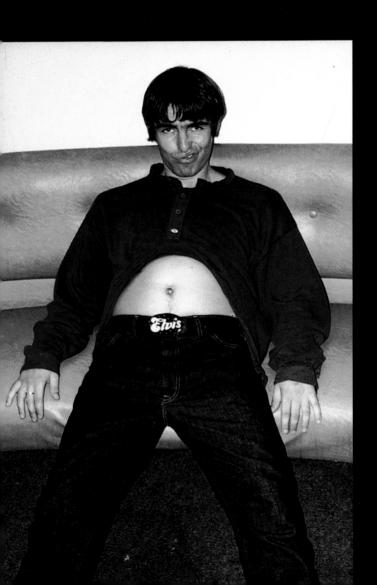

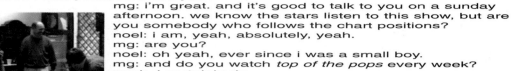
it's sunday evening about 6:50p.m. and a group of friends assembles at noel's house. the radio is tuned to 98.8fm. it's radio 1 and mark goodier is doing the chart rundown.

mg: take that slides to the number 2 position. and with that news we make a phone call. hopefully, noel gallagher from oasis is on the phone. noel are you there?
noel: i am, yeah, how are you?

mg: i'm great. and it's good to talk to you on a sunday afternoon. we know the stars listen to this show, but are you somebody who follows the chart positions?
noel: i am, yeah, absolutely, yeah.
mg: are you?
noel: oh yeah, ever since i was a small boy.
mg: and do you watch *top of the pops* every week?
noel: i certainly do.
mg: what would you like to be in the chart today?
noel: well, i'm not sure, it'll be wherever our wonderful fans have put us. i wouldn't like to say really, but hopefully number one, but if it's not, if it's not, you know ...

mg: you think it could be number one. i can now confirm that it is the highest new entry. you've actually knocked take that off the top: you are number 1, noel.
noel: well, it feels good. i'd just like to say thanks to all the people that bought it, especially the fans—all the people that came to sheffield as well. thanks a lot.
mg: congratulations! oasis debut at number 1, here it is, the new chart-topper, "some might say."

it was the band's first no.1 and celebrations went on long into the early hours. even the krafty kiwi, alex, was known to toe the line that night.

the video shoot for "roll with it" was shot in a studio in kings cross. a highly "creative" video director uses a gyroscope to film the band. yah. like rolling with it, right. "i'm not going on it, whatever the fuck it is." at the height of the blur/oasis chart battle it doesn't matter about videos. the song pisses all over the competition anyway. you might win the battle, but you may not win the war.

wonderwall video shoot, august '95

cool as fuck. armani leather, burberry
shirt, perfect bangs, ice-blue eyes,
the kid looking the don.

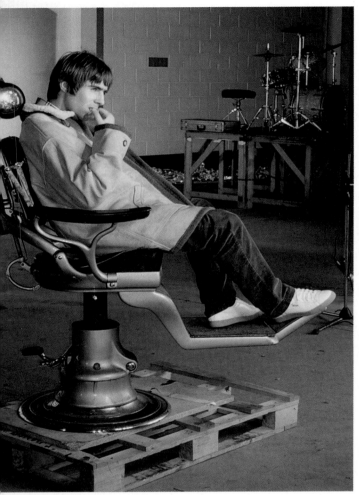

rockin' in my rockin' chair

oasis' first major network tv show
in the states on america's then-
rising star of talk shows. last to
perform, the band sat and
watched other guests do their
thing, including scott bakula, star
of *quantum leap*. after this tv
show the band made a quantum
leap in america themselves.

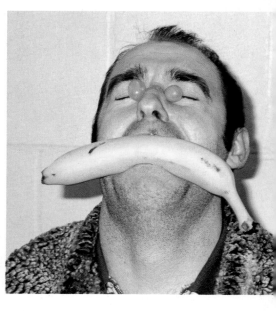

sticky fingers—the little piggy's played—c'mon.

PUBLIC ENEMIES
would you let them onto your
manor?

liam loses his passport at
canadian/american custom point.
anything to declare? "yeah! I'm
raving and mad for it."

the green room, david letterman show, '95

walking, baiting, berating, quaking, rocking and rolling, moving and shaking

where norman wisdom meets lou ferrigno
meets carling out of scum meets ... fuck off,
dick

pitch invasion. noel in new frontman recruitment shock.

"there's a dwarf on stage and he's nicked the tambourine."
"you're off your tits. here, have another toot."
"hang on a minute it's digsy, or someone smaller."
"well, he's got to be a scouser with that shirt and them kecks."

we're mods ...

... casuals ...

... indie schmunglists ...

... but definitely ...

... punks ...

... drunk ...

... not skinheads ...

... hats off, a number three suits you sir.

japan. honorable japan. guigs salutes his rising sons.

liam: "this is for all the fuckin'
silly long-haired people at the
back smokin' silly cigarettes."
coming on to the verve's
"northern soul," the chief
breaks into "swampsong" with
the greeting from liam, "better
than blur any day." the
ley-lines converge from the
lost weekend. robbie williams
absconds from take that and
beckons to the impromptu call
from the kid to large it. (rob ate
my hamster pose.) noel later
reveals on his radio show on
GLR that it was part of "the
masterplan." fired for good. it's
proper!

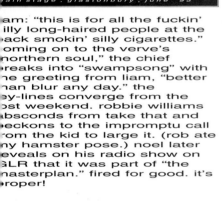

"hats off to you all—c'mon the
kids."
liam greets the crowd. smaller, cast
and the verve (rip) support.

digsy and steven from smaller get signed up to better records, witnessed by famous frontman after supporting him at leicester's de montfort hall. liam becomes tour manager for their tour — last seen catching a ride on a garbage truck after the roadhouse, manchester gig at 3a.m. sunday morning.

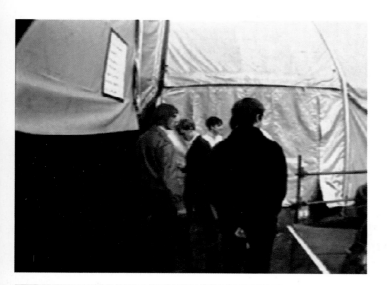

phoenix festival , stratford-upon-avon , july '95

ON-STAGE

Stage: Main

Name: Noel

No. 3512

straight after
irvine, noel
and myself fly
down to the
phoenix festival.
noel is to guest
with the rt. hon.
paul weller and
co. top thumper
steve white and
the ocean colour
scene boys make it
a right old family
affair.

god and the mod

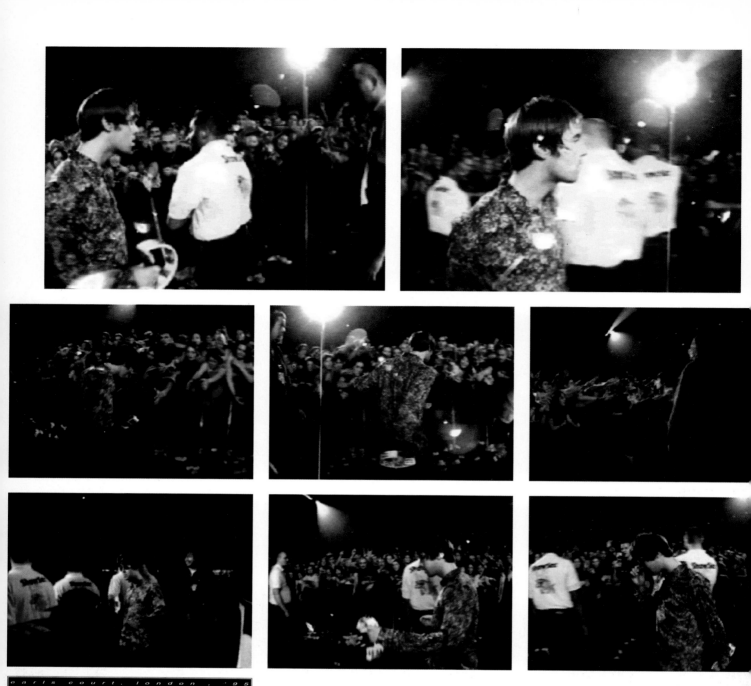

earls court, london, '95

like a champagne earl's court supernova

om seeing oasis playing
 eight people only two
ears before, to the largest
door gigs ever played in
is country. caught
etween a landslide in a
hampagne earls court
upernova. the size of the
enue, the stage set, the
rings and brass. looking
wn on a sea of 20,000
eople bringing it on down.
notions electric
elings electric
ve it to me—two time.

the biggest gate of the season for city. the kippax stand had never seen so many kippers (faces) and a fitting homecoming for the burnage boys. as the blues went down that weekend, the band went up into the stars, their faces projected on huge screens putting them alongside the ranks of their peers. rock legends. onwards and upwards; no stopping, never had been. end of an era, beginning of a new era. it's going off … all around the world. spread the word.

as the sun sets on maine road, the lights go out in los angeles. as a new morning rises over a blacked-out downtown, the methedrine mile of hollywood ends fortunes for some and starts them for others. the boy from burnage reinvented himself to produce the world-conquering "what's the story." instead of las vegas, next time around he chooses the idyll of mustique to care for the ones he loves and regroup his thoughts to write number three. three years, three albums—maybe four—the masterplan. all around the world—we are going to be the biggest band in the world— **BELIEVE**—definitely.

it's gettin' better man!